ENGLAND'S GREEN

ZAFFAR KUNIAL

England's Green

faber

First published in 2022
by Faber & Faber Ltd
Bloomsbury House
74–77 Great Russell Street
London WC1B 3DA
First published in the USA in 2022

Typeset by Hamish Ironside
Printed in the UK by TJ Books Ltd, Padstow, Cornwall

A CIP record for this book is available from the British Library

ISBN 978-0-571-37679-7

With thanks to Douglas Caster and University of Leeds,
University of Manchester, Manchester Metropolitan University,
Manchester Literature Festival, Brontë Parsonage Museum,
The Oval and Places of Poetry, and to many others
who know who they are.

4 6 8 10 9 7 5

as ever
for my son
and in memory of my mother

Contents

PART II

OUT

PART I

I N

In full magic –
        – TED HUGHES, 'Fairy Flood'

En: proto-Indo-European root of *in*
अनृतर * (antar)
interior, inside, margin, spacing, interval,
(by extension, figuratively) soul, a secret,
hidden thing

Foxglove Country

Sometimes I like to hide in the word
foxgloves – in the middle of *foxgloves*.
The *xgl* is hard to say, out of the England
of its harbouring word.
Alone it becomes a small tangle,
a witch's thimble, hard-to-toll bell,
elvish door to a door. *Xgl*
a place with a locked beginning
then a snag, a *gl*
like the little Englands of my grief,
a knotted dark that locks light
in *glisten*, *glow*, *glint*, *gleam*
and Oberon's banks of *eglantine*
which closes in on the opening
of *Gulliver* whose shrunken *gul*
says 'rose' in my fatherland.
Meanwhile, in the motherland, the *xg*
is almost the thumb of a lost mitten,
an impossible interior, deeper than forests
and further in. And deeper inland
is the gulp, the gulf, the gap, the grip
that goes before *love*.

Forget-Me-Not

A heart-note whispered into the ear of a mouse
disappearing and delicate
which was how you felt
when the house was a shudder, loud downstairs
and you shut your door against it
shouldering a broken world
in your shirt, primary-school light blue.
So much to come, I would quietly say to you
from inside you, each syllable
a lifetime away. And in a way I do.
I am.

The Hedge

This place is full of them. England. Britain.
Its green envelope. Hedges. Or the unflagging
unflappable ghost of hedges, at the shore
of eyesight or running along the kerb.
Thorned blank verse, strange runes, folioed text.
What is behind the same hedge from one day
to the next can be from entirely elsewhere.
Perhaps another time. A bewitched curtain.
I know the scratches that come from seeking

the lost in a hedge. Scratches you didn't know
were happening. The unexpected denseness,
the unexpected release. From the dark thicket
of light. It was today's light, I think, that pulled
an old hedge out of thick air's sleeve, and with it
a disappeared wicket, a Springfield Street,
a book with cursive black swords, a satchel,
a bricked-up church door, a truant morning,
perhaps Birmingham, perhaps the whole of unknown

England and beyond.

This in Land

That way a butterfly lifts an edge of world
is this horse chestnut tree going nowhere.

That way thunder feels bright and dark
is this moss, lit from under earth up.

That way the tip of a rosebud buries the future
is this stone smell unpronounced before rain.

That way a star's ground is mineral
is this steeple pointing down in the pond.

That way *this* ends, or doesn't with the word
is that way I am earthed by a hand.

England

History is now and England
– T. S. ELIOT, 'Little Gidding'

We all have lives that go on without us.
I've a cricket-me who didn't stop – like that
was that, when my bat had felt as heavy as England
and I took no wickets while the coach stood in my net
in the second and final trial for Warwickshire.
A bear and staff on my jumper, perhaps later . . .
But those butterflies. It thundered outside
on that second day. Life forks and stops
where another follows on. England's Moeen
Ali went to my school. His dad's from Dadyal.
Mine's up in the village over the bridge.
I don't know if he knows what I do now.
Dad I mean. We all have lives that go on
without us. Unwritten. I have history on grounds

I've not played on. Grace Road. The Oval. Eden
Gardens. We all have lives that go on without
us. It matters where the line breaks. I knew
I should pursue this future – that was almost
behind me, at the woods' edge, a realm between
weathers, where losses and times fold, at the crease –

clueless as to what it was. Or for whom.

Green

after Juan Ramón Jiménez

Green she is when I find her. Or find her grave. A second
time. I saw but didn't look at the life in the front garden
on the way to the church, never mind the little nameplate
which had lost its stick and been driven to a back wall
towards her garden, on the green tide of a mower, I guess.
I found it unexpectedly. Slate grey. She who taught me how
black shapes tame sounds – A is for acorns, apples. But why
is this grass so green? And what are you doing here?
I keep asking, over the grass. Over jungles and over seas
from bedtimes when my father worked. *Nights.* The word
hid a job, the dark's factory. *Not there, not there,* she says
as I feel the seeds out from a sunny packet and lob them over
the lawn she'd kneel on, a decade later, losing hours to find
a four-leaf clover I'd take into exams at the end of corridors
– but no, the nasturtiums should go in the border. Wake
Green Road, where Tolkien lived and saw his Old Forest
move, was off my road, a road that led to the hospital
I was born in and nearly was not, small, blue, having a fit.
When we left home one Christmas day, it was because
I wouldn't wear a paper crown from a cracker and Dad
exploded. To him the green hat was a country, unfolded –
a flag I didn't see. The mostly missing forest of Arden
marched on in moss and hard gaps. Hard as baked conkers.
Concrete. Like the dread, older than life, that was always
her death. Solid. In a hole in the ground. It was here – in
Bodenham, in the Welsh Marches, miles from the choked-
up ring roads, a grey concrete tide, the locked stone wreath
of motorways and my patch of city, with that small grass
roundabout branching like a mad clock to Moseley
village, Hall Green, Sparkhill, Sarehole – we held

her wake at England's Gate. Of all places. A coach
house country pub, a bus stop away from this grave.
Bus in our house meant *enough*, which I took as *stop*
as tea poured from a green spout. I'll stare further on
not looking at the front garden as I pass, as I stare now
at this green hair, cut grass, the loose nameplate I press in,
remembering those seeds, a round nasturtium, a thin cosmos.
Her laughing at me as I threw their promise in the lawn.
Between buses I feel the lock of the hour. *Not there,
not there*. However short the life that began with her
a green gate will always open from a hinge in the air.
Unlatched like this now

Invisible Green

was always there. Against the cold waving spires
of London grass, painted iron Victorian spears
point above. As they should they disappear.

Shade of far landscapes. Now your eyes are leaves
in a Yorkshire wood, all that was good, it lives
on. In and past the hard railings, love

Invasive

[Thunder. Enter the three Witches] . . .
First Witch: *A sailor's wife had chestnuts in her lap*
– WILLIAM SHAKESPEARE, *Macbeth* (1606)

1616

Sweet chestnuts from the Romans, but this whole land, till
now, is devoid of the horse chestnut tree – a giant green bell
of a gap – which broadly comes, like our proto-Indo-European
tongue, from candle-flowered kingdoms around the Black Sea.
This spring, Shakespeare is buried near his birthday – April
clapping exact earth either side of his life – and this same year

sailing from Turkey in the silky, spiky purse of the future
conker trees land here, with invisible strings, like fate

[Enter William the Conqueror]

1066

After an endless wait (How long is a piece of breeze?)
at the end of September, the northerly winds abate.
William crosses the Channel, puts a first foot on broken
English shells. He falls flat on the shingle. History in pieces.
Not the script. The king to be grips fistfuls of sand – dark
gaps above shale – behind him sails flap huge leaves

on the waves, a moving forest of masts. The Normans
bite their lips – till the conqueror barks:

*Sailors, it's fate we'll take this kingdom – I grip
already earth of this island!* English sand

falls, this minute, from his fingers and thumb, which
widen to cheers from the masted sea, where ropes
hang plumbline straight. Five digits of his hand
cast a shadow leaf. Meanwhile time gallops.

Shapes. Spreading from the future on the beach.

Foregrounds

for Raqib Shaw

I

One collected begonias,
and was tempted by bonsai trees
but worried that their tray world
was too shallow and cruel.
My other grandfather – never met,
even more short-lived – wouldn't wear
shoes. Survived only three days
after a small snake found a foot.
Mohammed Said. The name reads
in English like a sentence cut.

II

One can't own such old bonsai, a Kashmiri
artist says, in his opulent London patio
occupied by ancient trees, and by potted begonias
that temporarily move me to a Warwickshire garden.
Grandad's house. Next door, behind pots, a family
of Shakespeares. Sunday visits to England
from England. But this tree before me, this
hugely expensive bonsai pine, even in Kyoto
would stand out. Its four-hundred-year-old sigh.
Its Himalayan air. The thin soil's slight incline

to the pronounced tree foot moves a mountain
to here. If an exile's sigh has a word, or sign,
for me it's *such*. Such. A custodian of potted
histories, of what has passed beyond reach
or owning. In my father's house, the word *such*
means 'true'. Said at the sad, far end of a sigh,
followed by a cigarette drag. On hearing a fellow
from his thinned, mountainous land say 'Life is short'
or 'That's how it is'.   A sigh. Then: 'Such.'   'Such.'
I'd wait. Nothing. Such *what*? I'd think. Such *what*?

I return to look at the four-centuries-old bonsai
pine. A trunk of wounded rings, collecting inches
from each owner's time. I stare, now rooted to
the spot, to what I couldn't let pass. An old flinch,
wanting to correct or prune my father's version
of Himalaya. He said the end like the clipped end
of Cordelia. The *a* before – the syllable I'd trim
at the heart, he drew out as aahhh: *Himaahhhlia*.
It ends: *a layer*, I'd think. Later I'd see better. Four
syllables. Himalaya. All his. And one I say as *Him*

Thinnings

In the last light he saw the flowers closing up; and <u>he saw</u>
<u>the wood leopard</u>, which had left the leaf where Mischa
had placed it and was walking on the path. <u>Rainborough</u>
<u>watched it for a moment or two and then he ground it</u>
<u>under his heel.</u>

       – IRIS MURDOCH, *Flight from the Enchanter*
        (underlinings made in 1969, in purple,
         in my mother's copy of the novel)

Moonlit dust, gather
with each *mote*, death's weight – take wing.
Make off, small mother.

    *

Mute sunbird. Living
gerund. Stemless flower-
ing. Soul thing. Thinning.

  * * * * * *

In weeping willow
Wood Leopard, black and white, un-
readable as air.

    *

Holly Blue . . . margin
haunter – through life's sharp hedge – your
thin flame keeps going.

    *

Clouded Yellow – blur
in the laburnum – old dim
light I remember.

*

You belong between,
Pale Mottled Willow – whether
this world, or that one.

*

Blotched Emerald – there,
past the hospital curtain,
far off, off kilter.

*

Your mark wasn't thin –
Purple Hairstreak, oak lover –
but wide. Dark lightning.

*

Green Hairstreak hovers –
Mum waves a gift, found again –
my four-leaf clover.

*

Ghost Swift – underwings,
flash your white, underwrite our
long disappearing.

*

O *Dingy Skipper*,
wobbly captain, sailing
oakbrown and sombre.

*

_in__ ___ er _in __ ____ er _in __
____ er . . . look, above, a _in__ ___ er
partially hidden.

*

Through pockets of air,
that sheer see-through magician –
here, gone – *Small Copper*.

*

Green-Veined White's odd inn-
er light. Nettle and phosphor.
No stranger dyeing.

*

Small Heath reappears
in closed, shy brackets of wings:
(my dad once lived there).

*

. . . nettles, willow, elm,
. . . in hops, on rocks, walls, *Comma*,
don't stop, carry on

*

By the grave, a new
Satin Beauty is leaving
the thicket of yew.

Pressings

Rushing down the hill the signs are the same.
At the end of Birchcliffe Road comes Birch Place
which for the nth time I read as Birth Place.
So many years, so many miles from my first room,
though the way the trains work now nothing's that far.
Who'd have thought the future would be this, that we'd
travel, pitched like music, dark matter, through
solid walls? Soon I'll be at the station, and back
in my first room's unnerving foothold. Once,
barefoot among toys, I shuddered. First thought
(somehow pre-verbal): what's under my toes?
Second thought: I've stepped on a needle. Third:
the metal is HOT. After lifting my foot,
it took an instant before word and warm instinct
caught up with the worlds beneath me . . . *wasp*.
Dead. But not. I'd think of it when steel touched
vinyl and old beginnings revolved. Once,
Paul's voice, in the desert of mono, shouting
fOUR – as in one-two-three . . . – was my dad,
downstairs, calling ZafFAR, far past the closed
door. There were times it wasn't my name but dOOR
– as in Oi, close the . . . – but it *is* shut I'd think,
turning, each time. Another disc, another planet.
'This is a stereo recording.' I stare then and now

at the sleeve. Around a drum, a crowd of stars.
Yogis, gurus, cut-out faces, Einstein, Dors,
Jung, Wilde, Marilyn Monroe, Dylan Thomas,
Fields, Lawrence of Arabia, Sri Yukteswar
who looks like Dad and Sir Robert Peel, who
I'd seen as a kid in Mum's birthplace, Tamworth,
a monument, ignorant of its patience or the lengths
it would go to. Once, I put a pin on an atlas –
ruled a line – between Mum's birthplace
and Dad's. The exact centre would hold my start,
I'd decided. The dot fell in the Black Sea.
I lowered the needle once more on *Sgt. Pepper* . . .
a black hole at the heart – and it begins. *silence*
violins tuning, *unseen audience*, *a hum* –
the sound of background cosmic radiation.
A drum, a drum. At the start was the densest dot,
there was not even an around, round this heavy
inward sharpness – thousands of times more hot
than the sun's centre – a crescendo reversed,
so compact you could pin the light down, perhaps.
Or light's first, closed, bedroom door . . .
I've arrived at the station, thinking how birth
is the A-side to death's B-side, and how fast
we travel, these days – dematerialised – gone –
reshaped elsewhere. A cloud of cosmic dust
or butterfly soup, not winged nor crawling –
indefinite, unpressurised atoms, going in
and out of spheres. Each scattered bit of *me*
reprised to act one – that big act – as one.
The act you've known for all these years.

Wings

They're there. To the side.
It's hard not to stare
at the centre of the screen
and the mournerless funeral
or whatever black hole
the news has come to cover,
masked. But look beyond the edge
to what's felt in the wings, off
screen, keenly aware of the hour,
keener than ever, because stood

elsewhere. And when you
have followed a day's allowance
going alone into the new now,
but no phone, no camera,
no zoom, down the narrow
path into the soon
owl-haunted Nutclough Woods –
stepping over limb-like roots and dips
and glooms on this steep sloped
hill of a day – even still, look

to the verges. Where some distant
pixel-flowered plant – nursing summer
and its weakest blue, a touch smaller
than a forget-me-not – takes hold
at a sharp corner of the descent, like a note
to the self, or the snag of a passed-on
meme, a snatch of viral advice
from more crowded times. Down

there, through the scrolling
of a fern's frayed edges. *Look* . . .

Ahead – on the crumbling shelf
of a path that goes on, like the hour
or like the misted arm of a cedar.
And on the wing of a sheer drop
and by a few millimetres of earth's grace
each blue head is held, holds –
this anonymous brightness
that's almost not there, by the wayside
unmagnified. *Look for the helpers.*
They're there. They're there.

Cocooning

Word, I keep reaching for –
crossing you out, and then
putting you back in – *and*
this unhinged monastical spring

where I see nothing pass from hand
to hand, save between these two
like the different inhalers I carry
in every room – there are four

of them here, inhalers I mean,
each shaped the same, like a day
with its own shade of breeze, colour –
it's good to have you, *and*

staring distantly, at a locked summer,
the ongoing – you're a cell's window,
the old stained glass I open, to say
then and *then* and *then*

The Nonsense of Observing Outer Space

This butterfly comes from a bud
they call the small cocoon
it occupied before it was
this speckled, flitting bloom.

Back in that darkly shrunken space
it breaks down cell by cell.
Now, liquefied, its black-holed eyes
gape past that pupal gel:

that dense and nascent universe
that spooled our sent-out star.
This point that bore that point before
flaps storms to Palomar.

Bascote Heath, Long Itchington

I see. This is the shape remembrance takes.
To get it, the scale had to be brought home.
Picture the dead *moving in one long continuous*
column, four abreast . . . as the column's head
reaches the Cenotaph the last four men
would be at Durham. In India, that column
would stretch *from Lahore to Delhi.* Whichever
the country, it would take three and a half days,
this snaking march, before the tail caught up
with the head. Somewhere on the way you'd find
two who share a strand of my DNA.
So here I am, standing at the Cenotaph,
a century on, the centre of London.
To my eyes, this column seems made of limestone,
dense skeletal fragments of coral and shell.
Returning to that long, imagined march,
you'd be somewhere in the Midlands, I'd guess,
between London and Durham – perhaps Bascote,
where you, *Lance Corporal Albert Evetts*
of the Royal Warwickshires, were born – born
in Bascote, killed near Basra, and unburied,
like your son, killed somewhere at the Somme,
Private Roland Evetts of that 1st battalion
which braved no man's land in the Christmas truce.
Who knew? In your local church I found you,
on opposed pages, in a memorial book –
I first spotted your names behind the altar
in Long Itchington. I'd gone to Warwickshire
for graves, armed with my mother's maiden name –
3 and a half football teams someone has added

in blue biro. Now, in London, what I'm reading
doesn't say much. But this isn't weathering
where soft limestone loses letters, or mosses
names. It wants to be plain. THE GLORIOUS DEAD.
Repeated. Either side. And all else is blank
but for Roman numerals. Your upright coffin.
I see the whole thing as a numeral now –
one, *I*, call it what you will. This upright
cenotaph. On the 1911 census,
I found you both, under one roof. Father
and son: *limestone quarrymen*. I see you, arms
raised in unison, hacking down at the stone,
driving a wedge into the slab. Now. And now
on this kerbed island, I've been here for two
hours, moved and fixed as a capital's traffic
passed. I've heard the bells of Big Ben twice.
I want to cross over, to home in on the peak
of your empty tomb, but cars and cabs strand
me for now a long way from where you set
out, at this stone column that stands for you –
this *I* – that I've been stood here speaking to.

Ings

I've come back to a place called Ings.

Not that I ever stopped or noticed the signs to slow.
On autopilot, I breezed through a fast, straight road where
the Lake District becomes Yorkshire, and was twice caught
by speed cameras – in the mirror, the flash disappearing

behind me, unbelievably, in both directions, on different days.
I couldn't have been more exactingly clocked, there, in Ings

while less meaningfully there. And still there, points on my
licence and that afternoon in a hotel at a speed awareness
course in Kendal. That bright patterned carpet. I'll visit Ings

one day on purpose, I kept silently saying.

Ings. The name came to mean: Now. Slow. Down. And little
else. A splash of houses cut by a dual carriageway, a petrol
station, a lane with an easily missable church. Years after,
I'm walking

on the A591, south of Windermere station. Cars thunder
beside me. Tall noises. It's raining.

An incomplete word, ings.

Acres of wet. Marshy ground. Like grief, I think as I step,
past the phone box, through the gate and into the graveyard
at St Anne's Church. *Ings*

I am in you, I write in the imaginary visitors' book of the air. Behind me the tall speed cameras on the central reservation, their flashes of lightning.

Snowdrops like streetlamps, heads very down. Small ghosts of mourners round the stones. This stone is an open book. On the recto page, MEMORY OF. But I see the verso page first, and stare at IN LOVING

as though the words stood alone, in a separate world from the other side. Walking past snowdrops, I can't unsee this sentence on these wet little books. IN LOVING.

IN LOVING.

In the blowy wet distance a yew, shivering.

Mercifully, the door wasn't locked. It opens into the dark. In the belfry I can make out a rope, a ladder. Through the next door, in the quieter light, walls are freshly coated, and window colours bright, though some of the words on the stained glass feel stern. *Be not faithless but believing.*

From the outside, a leaded stained-glass window looked dull as a marsh fritillary's wing.

On a new chair, inside, I'm drying out, eating bread and cheese. Dead time, they call it, where nothing can be done. Nothing or numbness or silence presses down on my shoulders. I stay with it, or it stays me. Quixotic as the small church, time, with its oddly mixed plans, was passing.

I'm reminded of a slim book, *A Month in the Country*. It's the film's vision, though, I see, a 1980s filtering of a summer in 1920. Perhaps because it's raining

when the steam train pulls in. A shellshocked character in
Yorkshire loses his stammer as he hears hymns from the
graveyard – *God, what God? There is no God!* – before he
swallows it back down. I must continue, I'm digressing.

There is something

locked-in about grief, but there is something

horribly unlocked about grieving.

Before I leave the empty church, I pull the rope slightly and
feel a rung of the ladder. I'm climbing

now. Opening

now the trapdoor above the dark entrance. On the first
scaffold the bell tower is brighter, another dimension.
Tins of Farrow & Ball paint on the decking.

Another level now. And another. Dry weather blows into
the tower. *Ings*

I am really in you, I say, inwardly. Reaching

out from a high rung – I touch the huge cold bell. It doesn't
budge. Arm out, it feels like I am touching

Time. Pushing against a broad, cast stillness. In the realm
above, the dusty sound of cooing

fluttering.

My weight between the holding ground of a rung, and the
higher unringing

bell, I was tiptoeing

shaking.

Beside the church grounds, I put my hand on a wall by a
stream that drowns out the dual carriageway. It's only light
now that rains, upwards. Light, shaky as I am, a breeze of
light. Little steepling

points of memory I could tune out of and into. Swaying

gleams like the tips of buds on an early willow, but the tree
long gone, detached from its day, only the glints left, light
thickening

into what? A face? And there, howling

grief, or feeling

fought back, feeling

too big for the moment to hold, then the same person
walking

in, smiling

in a changed weather. Faces, at weddings

funerals. Flashpoints in a life. Budding

leaving.

Willow leaves of light on the water that flee or return. A kind
of us in the air, dilating

disappearing.

A thousand summers in winter. No. Words will not do.
The gleams are over before the word is through. Either way,
I tuned out of these gleams, or them out of me, and I left.
Left through the graveyard, past the stones with carved
words that still stopped IN LOVING

IN LOVING

and leaving

where I arrived, past the gate, and the call-box, and the snow-
drops – tiny tongueless bells – the quietness is still ringing

despite the cars on the loud road. Hours later, hours north
of Ings –

between Grasmere and Easedale – nearer the far tipping-

point of spring

a kestrel is overhead. In the wind it circles, carrying its own
turbulence. For a wide-winged moment, the bird is still, as if
nested in the eaves of the wind or pushing

against the edge of an unseeable force that stops things

short or holds things

in. Life, within life, continuing

PART II

OUT

*I was a hidden treasure, and I wished
to be known, so I created a creation*
— Hadith

*When there is nothing in common between the dream
thoughts, the dream work takes the trouble to create a
something ... The process is analogous to that of rhyme,
when consonance supplies the desired common factor*
— SIGMUND FREUD

Ex Nihilo

There was an Old Lady whose folly
Induced her to sit in a holly
— EDWARD LEAR

An impulse in the night snow
draws her like a nail to the evergreen oak –
the armoured, angular holly –
to lean back

against its medieval gravity –
tight weaponry that might have been
time's own prickling fabric – now
the holly spikes

take the weight of her coat, her dress, her body
and, yes, soul – a thousand pins she can sense
sharp and yet benign, shielded as she's borne
for a beautiful clock-

less time, her whole self, cushioned on the green
couch, the shocks to come a kind of air
she rests on, through thin and thick
as snowflakes

and stars and all her lives are there, fully present
on the holly, until tears appear – not tears
that chime with Lear, but deep cuts
to a very real fabric

the real nonsense being
that nothing is everything
at stake.

Unland

Meet me at the bridge: I'll take you to your parents.
– Spirited Away

I

press on, and lean into it: where the line
stops, rhododendrons stare. At the cold air
past the proverbial wardrobe. Portals unlitter
the place. A ball you were chasing as it climbs
under a grey cloud can vanish. Unland.
Leaving you more entire, but thinly there
like a photo against a painted background.
What else?   It's *ma.*   It's Japanese emptiness:

Scotch mist, absence in a clap. Between continents
a kingfisher cuts a blue gap. White moths. Haw
flakes. A snowflake, gone. The dark missing
step in a stair. A line in a film that goes
on beyond your watch. A hedge blinking.
Meet me at the bridge: I'll take you to your parents

No Face can tell
No Face knows you don't belong
in this world you've entered and are still
entering

No Face turns to follow yours
No Face can tell
through empty hungry eyes
a hunger that is eternal

and bottomless
holding your breath you cross
the bridge and No Face can tell
No Face can tell

Brontë Taxis

On the hour, up in the wind
I hear the parish chimes
and think of the word *parochial*
and then *precarious* –
the whole village almost clings
to the hill, as if stalled by the syllables
of a spell, a stopped fall, or rise –
the brunt air pulls at the branches
and reaches for foundations
and ropes, the high buried bells,
their tilting hinterlands –
precarious and parochial
the way whole islands can hang
on a vowel, windy
as an *o*, *u* or

e and how it all can turn – a land
found on the pebble of a *p* or a *b*
is lost in a high-browed, hawk-eyed *ë*
and I think of that low-rooted *y*
in the Ulster name *Prunty* –
a forked hawthorn at the end
of *border-country* – where wind
and earth, vowel and consonant
aren't continents apart – as the steep
B&Bs, their hinged signs
lifting in the breeze, grip the tipping
verticals of Haworth – here
within my radius in Brontë
Country – and a Kashmiri

cab driver puts his hand
to the gear, clutch down
up the cobbled road.

O'

And tricks frae magic Mac
– TAM WIGHT

are you watching closely
my great-grandfather Hugh
McDonald was a magician and a tap dancer
magic Mac's father Neil was an O'Donnell
who magicked his Donegal
surname Scottish after floating to Aberdeen
where he married a Julia Phinn
and their Hugh would in time run
an inn wherein he did his tricks
it is important to remember
magic Mac's mother was called Julia
as was her mother and you can forget for now
that her brother was a watchmaker
who lived one time in Dublin – now this second
Julia the elder Julia had a granddaughter
called Julia Phinn McDonald whose daughter
was called Julia who was English and was to be
my mother – here now is a coin magic Mac
pulled not from his coat pocket
but the small English ear of my eventual
mother – look it has two heads
here is his face – here is mine
ignore the three small round cups over
there and the floating o
in window or coat or poetry – forget
the world's shades coming through – keep
your eyes on this one coin
are you watching closely
are you watching closely

[42]

Scarborough

and when I got free of the town, when my foot was on
the sands and my face towards the broad, bright bay, no
language can describe the effect of the deep, clear azure
of the sky and ocean, the bright morning sunshine on the
semicircular barrier of craggy cliffs

         – ANNE BRONTË, *Agnes Grey*

I

Raised inland you were drawn towards our waves.
Like Mum, whose middle name was wrongly spelled
as 'Anne' on her last certificate. And your death
too – like that *e* – bothers me. Anne Brontë.
Quiet as castles, your grave, far from your Cornish
mum and Irish dad, is out, on a North
Sea limb. Banking on your life, ill, you'd go

east, days from your end – for what? The rub
of salty air? A picked-up pebble? And there,
the sea's drum, its unloosable knot, like the mum
cancer took early. The rhythm of memory
puts time ahead of itself and we're pulled to miss
a coast that is not yet home. The tide. It's an
oxygen machine, still going. Its constant hum.

II

Land is quiet under pressure. I can't bear
the long silence at the end. You have an *e* –
silent, stressed – ending your names. My mother's
mum began at a coast too – north, as the crow
flies, of you, Anne. Once, by a sea wall, standing
in the far southwest, St Ives – the other side
of your mum's birthplace, on that kicking foot

of Cornwall – looking at the Irish Sea, turning
to me, Mum said the tide was maternal, a comfort.
At five she lost her mother, Julia, to an asylum
and she'd never learn of the coasts before her.
If ever I asked, a silence, not quite hers, returned.
Perhaps I'll come back to this another time
and say more. Perhaps I'll speak again with you.

III

Inishowen. Shetland. Orkney. Have you seen a rock,
pocked by a limpet's coming and going, where home
gets spelled by scratches of a shell? Well. Guess what?
It's called a home scar. The Friday Dad met Mum
she was heading westward, for the coast of Rhyl
in north Wales and stopped off at Birmingham.
She was on her own and some force had pulled

her to the railway, to the sea. I get a pull to forget.
My local cinema. Under the hill,
my coast widescreens into view – loud waves, other
worlds lap in – my land's edge. Escape. Therapy.
Hebden Bridge Picture House. Near your start.
A red ceiling, ribbed. Whale's gut. Dark's womb.
Sea gusts or not, I don't care where action's set

IV

or when. Wherever I am I carry pebbles, Anne.
And shells. Small places, that open like a screen. Once
I placed pieces of one crystal on graves far
apart. I like films that go on, sagas. And. And.
I haunt the same seat. Other times are where
I watch beyond what happens, buried edgelessly
as a quiet last vowel. Inland and at sea.

*

I forgot to say, Mum was raised by her dad's
English parents. Who'd return to Rhyl
each summer. An Arthur. And an Agnes. Mum's
mother figure. Julia Ann was in delayed
mourning that Friday she took the train to sea.
There's extra things to say, as ever, but I'm
going to be quiet. And stop early. I'll

v

leave this here, Anne, wherever this is.

Hawthorn

I like it when memories aren't pinned
haughtily to words, but come to find
them, slowly on the bridge
of a warm breeze filled emptily
with blackbird songs, a robin
twisting its invisible screw
and a more piercing song
I can't yet name, and beside it a scent
that belongs at the slow start
of another summer, alive
and pungent and unattached
then to the off-white flowers
a little distance off from this bench
and the name, the name.

The Newly Bred Rose

'Rosa *Emily Brontë*'

When my nose hovered, close in,
the first thing, if *first* is the right word,
was tea. The smell of tea was an afterthought
impossibly, as though a fresh tablecloth
had been placed without disturbing the dusty
ancient books inside the front room, on the drop-
leaf table. After *tea* a new word started to form
tentatively, the way green wakes up
on a rose stem, like the bud
of a musk deer's antler pushing through
the head. Lemon perhaps. Guava?
Apricot? Beyond colour, on the spectrum,
I sense violet, far from the actual pink
which blushes yellow towards the stamen,
the centre. Scent is so primitive, sensed
in the reptile brain, shy of speech. Our earliest
preverbal stem. Yes, tea, certainly. No. Yes. And net
curtains, the way they trap old cloud
or what is dimly beyond them as the Cornish *haggel*
grips a hawthorn, and there's oak in the Old Irish *daur*.
There were no curtains in the house of before
but past the black front door now is this new rose.
Middle notes drawing on that mythical English summer
that always pitched further than the future. Over the hill
its heather, its weather. Coasts and their staggered
suns grafted together. Doorways made one.

Little Books

The universal God of [deletion] *might* [?]
– CHARLOTTE BRONTË, little book transcript

1. Gulliver's Travels

Charlotte, I'm remembering when you were
eight. I asked which of all books was dearest.
You answered right. Then like an Irish King
Lear to his daughter, I asked, *Next best?*
You said, *Father, it is the book of nature.*
I hold those stitched books in miniature
you and your sisters made. You, the last
I'd bury. Like your hidden, truer answer.
Never mind Bibles. In any seamed thing
or stone, lives, lands, stories, are crammed
like a wish for more world. For wings.
The weight of tiny books in my hand.
I see you dip into dark again. Gone.
And. And. And. And. And.

2. The Very Most Minute (A Small Ad)

Six young men wish to let themselves out
[+ ?] *hire for the purpose of cleaning out*
pocket[s] *they are in reduced CirCuMstanCes.*
I read *cleaning out* in its helpful sense:
lint, sand, fluff . . . Words have pockets.
Small, deep pockets that go on for ages.
We put words on a page and they preserve
infinitely more than we mean or guess –
a word minute as *in*, it turns out – even
the very most minute. We should advertise
to sort out the mess. I see magnified elves
in those *reduced CirCuMstanCes*, working
on next to nothing. The unseen impish stuff
that can seed a new land. Lint, sand, fluff.

3. *SOLD. BY NOBODY. AND PRINTED. BY HERSELF*

Bookbinder. The littler. Oldest. Older.
Littling pages for the fingers of a toy
soldier. You carry a hero's title. Nelson.
Duke of Bronte. North of Mount Etna.
Bronte, Greek *Thunder*. Shield carrier
for Zeus, or Jupiter, the child of Rhea
and Chronos, or Time. And later, after
these little books for the lead soldiers
you'd be Currer Bell, invisible, walker
in your new career. Hiding worlds in a
fogdrop. Littler. Speller. Courier. Carer.
The way griefs hide. In letters. Thunder
in foxglove bells. Littler. Than my mum.
Her stoneless grave. Teacher. Carrier on.

The Crucible

My grandfather was a ____ man, a quiet man
who went stonily quiet when his only child
decided to live with a man who wasn't yet
my dad. For a good three years, he held
firm, wouldn't speak to the daughter who wasn't
then my mum. When Abdul met Julia
in a Birmingham pub, Thunderclap Newman
were number one. *Call out the instigators –*
It took two weeks, Abdul staring at the number
and the dial – *Because there's something in the air.*
'Give Peace a Chance' was on its way to number
two. Ashamed of his accent in her dad's ear,
he delayed and delayed. But Julia, by the phone,
picked up on the first ring. It was summer,
the July of *one small step*. In Stratford-upon-
Avon, they had their first date, a good day until
Abdul said he was married with kids and Julia wept.
Years later I was born, three of us showed up
at his English door and the hard, long-kept
silence broke. The offered brown ale happened
to be one Dad knew and a Test match happened
to be on the grey box. Dad and Grandad hit
it off. Dad's relatives, abroad, would have seen
a clear way to hell through that dimpled beer
mug. Dad bawled at his funeral, as we threw dirt
into the hole. I was eleven, a number I won't
rhyme. An RAF sign on the red, white and blue
flag on his coffin. *Hand out the arms and ammo –*
History is now in boxes.
I'd glue Airfix

Spitfire wings, bit by bit – *We're gonna blast*
our way through here. Grandad lived like a hermit
after Julia left. His binoculars, bought for birds
and hardly out of the leather case, we turned
at the cricket. We kept his old pipe, which Dad
learned to like. I loved the length of its curved
stem, its earth smell, the scorched bowl shaping to
the hand, the moment. Gone to the four winds.
Two, a one-two-three-four! – I own Grandad's photo
of forty-seven airmen from the Second World War.
He's next to one of two brown men. In my one
family history box. Nothing from Dad's forebears
and no dates. Kala Khan. Jeevani. Ibrahim.
I love, too, odd names from my Warwickshire
quarter. Deeming. Hartshorn. Goode. Raven.
A favourite branch is where a Goode will marry
a Flamel in seventeen hundred and something.
Flamel whispers *flame*, altered stone, alchemy,
philosophy. And now – *Ev'rybody's talking*
'bout bagism, shagism, dragism, madism,
ragism, tagism, this-ism, that-ism, is-m, is-m . . .
in black and white, is a photo of my grandfather,
another only child, like Mum and Dad.
Stan is stood on stones the size of matchbuds.
Back turned, facing the sea, its sepia-grey area,
a Midlands boy in shorts, big waves I can't hear.
The war to end all wars was not long over
and in my hand, the shocked *now* of that tide,
its vast elemental shove, its endless shh

                          should

I say he wasn't good and became good,
should I be ashamed of him, who wouldn't
answer his daughter, those years he went cold
when Julia and Abdul weren't yet my parents

Empty Words

'they may not acorde' –
Chaucer's *Assemble of Foules* –
Parliament of Words.

*

The Speaker's habit
prolongs a vowel: 'The *aye*s have
it. The *aye*s have it.'

*

I would not accuse
anyone of misreading
big vowels like *U*s.

*

Clanging the zen gong –
is it ego, that I add:
Something keeps going

*

My father's Kashmir
ended with a smoky sigh –
its long rhyme with here.

*

Onland – opposite
of Offland. The capital
is shared, disputed.

*

Long hush. A good shout.
Give me this wait. Not the screen's
stone-cold OUT / NOT OUT.

*

Kant's *crooked timber* –
cricket bats can be English
or Kashmir willow.

*

In the beginning –
that middle was the spark – *or*
was the *Word*'s Big Bang.

*

Dad's word for 'and': *aur*.
More like *oar* – than *our* – as in
out at sea. And *or*.

*

Near Lahore, Dad's eye,
through smashed specs, met a firework.
Near Gloucester, King Lear.

*

Classic. Thought we'd be
a *Ulysses*, not, instead
'The Dead'. Long story.

*

Mr Palomar –
wore specs, like the deep space lens
flecked by dust and stars.

*

The Rat's small minute –
live 'By it and with it and
on it and in it'.

*

Prayer is not the words
but having none and staying.
Bell-less fairy weed.

*

look, love – a foxglove
hear the bee that hums within –
the *be* in forgive

Innings

A moment is like that, out of the hand
of the minute, the hour,
the planet clapping years together
and I only just get to the pitch of it,
feet indecisively placed, and out. Out.

Whereas I've seen Viv Richards bat
for a century, beyond – feet exactly where Grace
played at fifty – his eyes seeing the ball bigger
almost before its time, like another day's
light, knowing where it would land.

Daylight

short rectangle of you
on this confined floor
the lightest step to
the nowhere possible
less than an envelope
equal to its postage
stamp though faceless
o unstuck eye of light
sent anything anywhere
sends oceans sends faces
sends all but the sender

Leg Glance

Logos (n.) from Proto-Indo-European *log-o-,
suffixed form of root *leg- 'to collect, gather'

Flexing my knee, taking my guard
I looked up and spoke
in a breaking voice
'Middle and leg, please'.

There is a steadier me
who's always stood even further in the middle
at action's remove – mostly silent
in silence's own ground.

I know this from way back, for instance
facing a fast bowler off a long run and flicking
the ball from in front of my pads for
an eventual four

splitting the two fielders behind me
who run towards each other at the rope
in hope – for a small eternity –
the ball vanishing into a late May

hedge, its slow-time confetti dropping
ahead of early leggy foxgloves
their countless nodding wordless heads –
all of which I witnessed

as though I wasn't at the centre
of the echoing shot
as I pivoted slightly on one foot . . .
I say this but there was no word

in the beginning, no ligament of language
no lexicon at all – in that pool around
the shot I played
until I saw the scoreboard flap the change

and registered the clapping.

The Oval Window

Being *pitched* in stadia, walking out in the middle, there is a growing distance, as the crowd is further away, even loneliness but an intense presence surrounding you. This is what it can feel like writing alone, with – is it the atmospheric pressure of old, internalised words, distant voices, is it the idea of future hearers? – distant coasts. Is it one's *self*? A hum that is not yours thinks around you, rings into focus. From the middle ear to the inner. The witness within. The huge circularity, the international unknowable stadium of focus. Stretching before you and behind. The more you sense the needle – the gathered-round-you of the distant watchers – the more pressing the silence in a private bubble, private as an angel's trumpet, a hood, an intuitive, intimate intensity that the wider presence is feeding. An unstoppable outness, in. Out, in the middle.

The Groundsman

Since I retired, despite my runny hay fever
I love this long grass, gone to seed, green ears
left for ages that whisper to each other:
blue flax – a flagpoled can – a ragwort's wires –
foxglove spikes – shirty poppies – Queen Anne's lace –
a breeze with a beardy face – a crow feather –
a dotty cabbage white in a groundless shiver –
the alive among the dead in the fine chaos

of day. Its authorless sway of height and depth.
The charged haze its own kind of light brigade.
Rubbing my eyes I think of old work, each pitch
or playing field that blurs now into one flat grief –
grass shades that cross like ghosts, re-chalking lines
over decades where others have gone. Life

is wider than its page. And days are a cut field, clipped and made
    to run on.

Mid On

'Out, in the middle, far beyond
thoughts of being right, or wrong'
(Rumi is said to have said), 'there is a field' –

the Persian for such a square, or space, is *Maidan*.
I'd like to add, from my position, to that old
English field – 'I'll see you there', anon.

F

Following one world, another.
Within a withy, a willow thicket
I'd very much later recall the nets.
Winter nets every Saturday.
How they hung like a ship's sail.
And how one afternoon I truly saw
actual sails and felt the nausea
of a sea I'd never been on. A squall.
It was all centuries ago, I was surer
than ever. *Concentrate. Concentrate*
the coach was shouting in the indoor
nets while I looked towards but not at
the rows of mesh or windows beyond, after a stroke
I made sallied right into time's veils, into the shock
of an afternoon impossibly before
me, a sheer moment of rain on mast
and sail and deck. And a voice came
through thin weather, the thin end
of the future. *Let me see the maker's name*
facing forward at the end of the shot.
Strike through the line. Always present
the full face of the bat. Let me see the DF
on your Duncan Fearnley.
It's a good blade of willow, that.
I can only see the F. I can only see the F.

ANOTHER?

I know the feeling – of leaves at my head,
a spring behind, the pushy give of leaf and stem –
I'd seek it out as a child, four, six, ten,
without loss, a seat so particular I'd leave the small
weight of my shadow or shape and my mother would say
she could see, days after, the impression of my back,
my head, a growing dark where the bushy periwinkle
had flattened. Nameless then. There, with that first
springy sense behind me of being held, even loved
an inch or more above earth, cushioned by air
and that broken green hand and, and –
that scatter of purple-blue flowers – I'd stare
up, above this *sorcerer's violet*, this *joy-on-the-ground*
at the deeper blue adding upwards infinitely – and God
how far that word was from me – and wait till sky
flipped, till a sensation told me I could fall
up, and my legs would stiffen and twitch. Just then,
at the end of my coffee I saw separate shapes, letters:
A N O T H E R ? beneath the grounds, a cupped plea
to stay that leaves me unexpectedly emotional. I'd love
to know that ground-covering periwinkle was still there –
behind the house we left in a hurry, but finally this time,
leaving my father who's now left the land entirely –
offering its ivy-green give and lift, above earth, like this
coffee cup. If I could go back to that first garden
and if it were still there, that leafy planet,
my old staring seat, its matted mound
in the shade of the fence, the funnel-hearted
violet-blue stars, I would take it as proof of a holding on –
in the heaviest sense – and I know that I would lose it.

Snowdrop

The dead remember. Who said that?
I said that, said the dead. There is an
usness to everything. Every inanimate
who doesn't remember. You are merely
the muffled voice pushing. A berried yew
must crown me. Do not let the tide wash
the inner keep. This island is not dead.
What's the point of a dead bell? I am.

Over

it's nothing really
just the way it is
or was said on the heels of me
getting into my stride

that oval long held   *O*
then a lifted skyward   *ver* –
after the last short
drop of the stone in hand

to the white coat pocket
– I still hear   *O*   *ver*   *O*   *ver*
when no one's there
to say it

far from that pocketed day
lost to the weather
on a loud grey beach
taking a blind sole

step away from the creased
sea when my boot heel
knocks back a shell
or a whitened

pebble that might just
as well be a wisp or the lonely
thought that I haven't connected
with anything

The Wind in the Willows

Unread, the book was all shades of distance
but I knew the title and the title stuck. Mossy cover.
Hazed interior. The species too. I'd say, if asked,
it was my favourite kind of tree, though it was never
with one certain tree in mind. There was a garden

I vaguely remember, the way the leaves curtained
like shadows. A lit cave. A fringe, not yours, you could
look through. And the wood that grew by flowing water
carved cricket bats, which was a part of the little I also knew.
Maybe it was all a little to do with letters too, the tongueless

trees of that printed double *l*, or the uncrowing tall *W*s
of *The Wind in the Willows*; maybe it was all aural –
an echoed 'in', *Wind in* . . . the open-mouthed billowy *lows*
– maybe the leaf-fringed mystery, between the two.
And speaking of poetry, I had this initiating thought: in

the flax-smelling grain of the first bat I was gifted
wind was contained. Old power locked. A gravity well
beyond mine. Light enough, slight arms could lift it. Wind
in willow, this percussive wood a gathered strength. A mutual
bind. Though I was far from writing – or this book –

that sense, I suppose in spirit, was poetry and early.

The very last thing poetry is

is a poem.